D0919449

CUR
12/11

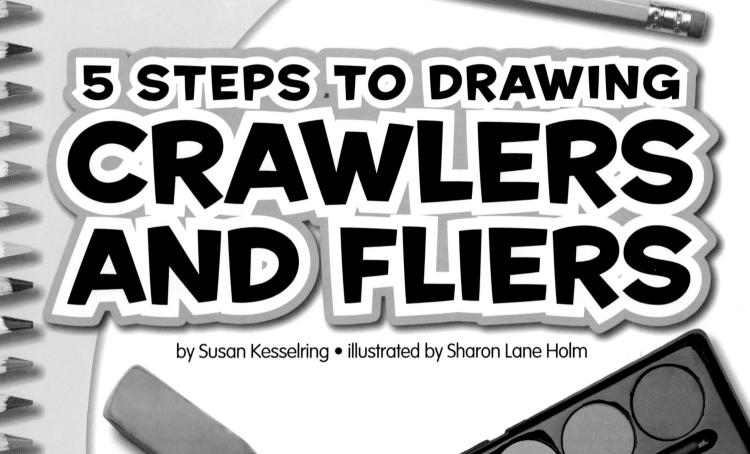

5 STEPS TO DRAWING
CRAWLERS AND FLIERS

by Susan Kesselring • illustrated by Sharon Lane Holm

Published by The Child's World®
1980 Lookout Drive • Mankato, MN 56003-1705
800-599-READ • www.childsworld.com

ACKNOWLEDGMENTS
The Child's World®: Mary Berendes, Publishing Director
The Design Lab: Design and production
Red Line Editorial: Editorial direction

Copyright © 2012 by The Child's World®
All rights reserved. No part of this book may be reproduced or utilized in
any form or by any means without written permission from the publisher.

ISBN: 978-1-60973-194-6
LCCN: 2011927702

Printed in the United States of America
Mankato, MN
July 2011
PA02088

TABLE OF CONTENTS

HELPING AND HARMING

Crawlers and fliers may be small. But the things they do make a difference in our world. Some of them eat other bugs that cause problems for humans. Ladybugs eat bugs that harm farm crops. Dragonflies eat pesky flies and mosquitoes.

Butterflies and bumblebees spread **pollen** that helps flowers grow. Ants help loosen soil and bring air into it. This makes the soil good for plants.

Asian long-horned beetles make a difference, too. But it's not by helping plants. The female beetle chews a hole through a tree's bark. Then she lays her eggs inside the hole. When the eggs hatch, the new beetles eat the wood of the tree. The tree will die if this goes on. Scientists are working to stop this pest from killing millions of trees.

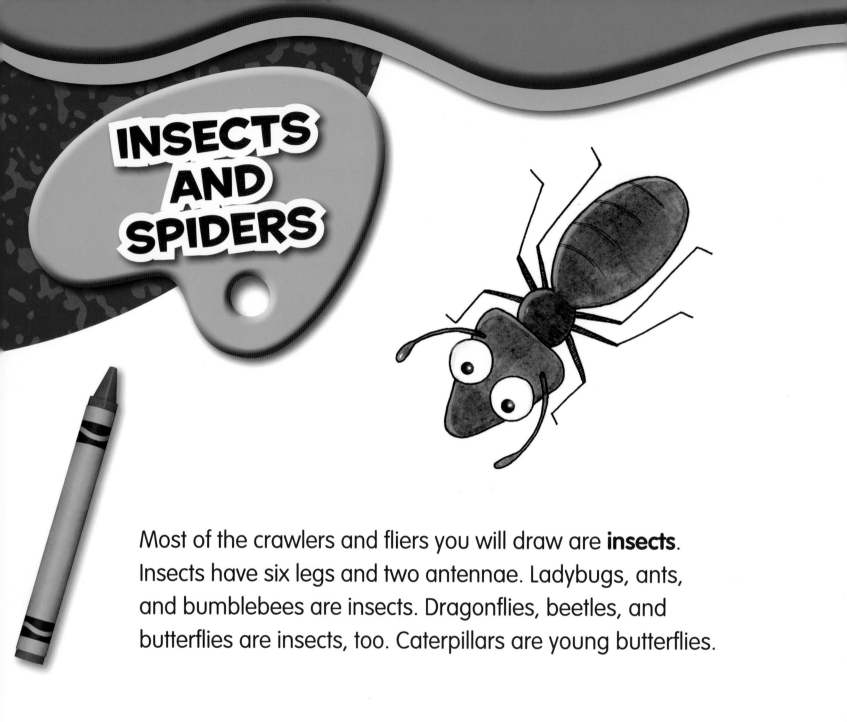

INSECTS AND SPIDERS

Most of the crawlers and fliers you will draw are **insects**. Insects have six legs and two antennae. Ladybugs, ants, and bumblebees are insects. Dragonflies, beetles, and butterflies are insects, too. Caterpillars are young butterflies.

Spiders are not insects. Spiders have eight legs instead of six. They have no antennae. Spiders can be black or very colorful.

STAGES OF LIFE

Butterflies, bumblebees, ladybugs, beetles, and ants go through four stages of life. They start out as eggs. When the eggs hatch, **larvae** come out. Most larvae look like small, white worms. Larvae eat and eat so they can grow into **pupae**. Pupae are usually found in **cocoons**. A pupa's job is to change into an adult insect.

Dragonflies and spiders have three stages of life. Dragonfly eggs hatch into **nymphs**. The nymphs live in the water for up to four years. When they are ready to become dragonflies, they shed their nymph skins. Then they are dragonflies. Baby spiders are called spiderlings. Spiderlings shed their skins many times before they become adult spiders.

DRAWING TIPS

You've learned about crawlers and fliers. You're almost ready to draw them. But first, here are a few drawing tips:

Every artist needs tools. To learn how to draw crawlers and fliers, you will need:

- Some paper
- A pencil
- An eraser
- Markers, crayons, colored pencils, or watercolors (optional)

Anyone can learn to draw. You might think only some people can draw. That's not true. Everyone can learn to draw. It takes practice, though. The more you draw, the better you will be. With practice, you will become a true artist!

Everyone makes mistakes. This is okay! Mistakes help you learn. They help you know what not to do next time. Mistakes can even make your drawing more special. It's all right if you draw the wings too big. Now you've got a one-of-a-kind drawing. You can erase a mistake you don't like, too. Then start again!

Stay loose. Relax your body before you begin. Hold your pencil lightly. Don't rest your wrist on the table. Instead, move your whole arm as you draw. This will help you make smooth lines. Press lightly on the paper when you draw or erase.

Drawing is fun! The most important thing about drawing is to have fun. Be creative. Your drawings don't have to look exactly like the pictures in this book. Try changing the position of the antennae. You can also use markers, crayons, colored pencils, or watercolors to bring your crawlers and fliers to life.

1

2
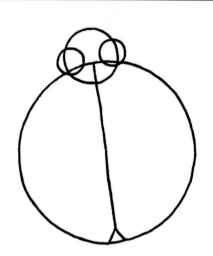

LADYBUG

3
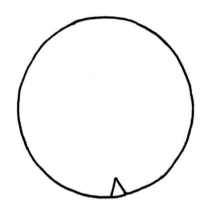

4
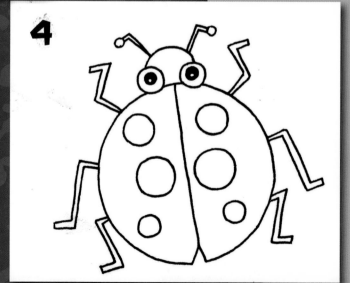

Ladybugs are known for their shiny, red wings and black spots. But did you know they ooze a stinky liquid when they sense danger? Their bright colors remind **predators**, "That one tastes bad!"

5

1

2

ANT

3

4

Ants are social insects. They do everything together. Ants "talk" with each other using smell and touch. They also send smell signals to warn of danger.

1

2

ASIAN LONG-HORNED BEETLE

3

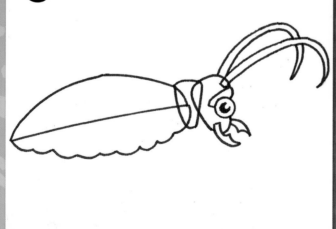

4

An Asian long-horned beetle is black with white or yellow spots. It has very long antennae. They have black and white stripes. The antennae help the beetle find the trees it wants to eat.

5

1

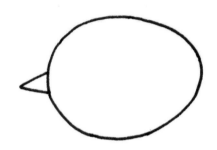

2

BUMBLEBEE

3

4

Bumblebees drink the **nectar** in flowers. They unroll their long tongues and stick them into the flowers to reach the nectar. Their tongues are hairy at the ends. The nectar sticks to the hairs.

1

2

SPIDER

3

4

Spiders make silk. They use the silk to build webs to catch their meals. They use silk to hold their eggs. The silk also helps them float through the air.

5

1

2

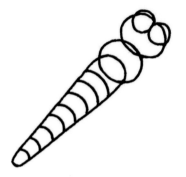

DRAGONFLY

3

4

People love the bright colors of dragonflies. Their fast, darting way of flying makes them fun to watch. They are also great at hunting mosquitoes.

1

2

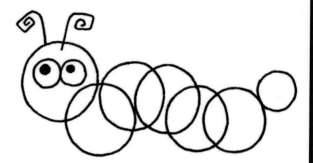

CATERPILLAR

3

4

Some caterpillars eat 27,000 times their body weight while they are growing. Sometimes caterpillars grow too big for their skins. They shed the old skins and leave them behind.

1

2

BUTTERFLY

3

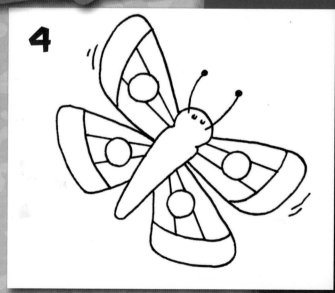

4

You know that butterflies are beautiful. But did you know that their bright colors help them stay alive? Bright colors show predators that butterflies would not taste good.

MORE DRAWING

Now you know how to draw crawlers and fliers. Here are some ways to keep drawing them.

Crawlers and fliers come in all different colors, shapes, sizes, and textures. You can draw them all! Try using pens or colored pencils to draw and color in details. Experiment with crayons and markers to give your drawings different colors and textures. You can also paint your drawings. Watercolors are easy to use. If you make a mistake, you can wipe it away with a damp cloth. Try tracing the outline of your drawing with a crayon or a marker. Then paint over it with watercolor. What happens?

Drawing Real Crawlers and Fliers

When you want something new to draw, just look outside. Do you spot anything moving on the ground? Look at the insect carefully. Is it big or small? Can you see how many legs it has? Does it have spots or a pattern? Now try drawing it! If you need help, use the examples in this book to guide you.

GLOSSARY

cocoons (kuh-KOONS): Cocoons are protective sacs for fertilized eggs. Caterpillars go into cocoons before becoming butterflies.

insects (IN-sekts): Insects are small creatures with three main body sections, six legs, and one or two pairs of wings. Dragonflies and beetles are insects.

larvae (LAR-vee): Larvae are insects in the life cycle stage between egg and pupa. Caterpillars are butterfly larvae.

nectar (NEK-tur): Nectar is a sweet liquid produced by flowers. Bumblebees drink nectar.

nymphs (NIMFS): Nymphs are young forms of insects that change into adults by shedding their skins many times. Dragonflies begin life as nymphs.

pollen (POL-un): Pollen is the powdery grain inside plants that helps make new plants. Bumblebees help spread pollen.

predators (PRED-uh-turs): Predators are animals that live by killing and eating other animals. Some insects are brightly colored to protect themselves from predators.

pupae (PYOO-pee): Pupae are insects in the life cycle stage between larva and adult. Pupae are usually found in cocoons.

BOOKS

Emberley, Ed. *Ed Emberley's Drawing Book: Make a World*. New York: Little Brown, 2006.

Regan, Lisa. *Bugs*. New York: Windmill Books, 2011.

Quick Draw: Creepy Crawlies. New York: Kingfisher, 2008.

WEB SITES

Visit our Web site for links about drawing crawlers and fliers:

childsworld.com/links

Note to Parents, Teachers, and Librarians: We routinely verify our Web links to make sure they are safe and active sites. So encourage your readers to check them out!

INDEX

ABOUT THE AUTHOR:
Susan Kesselring loves children, books, nature, and her family. She teaches K-1 students in a progressive charter school in Castle Rock, Minnesota.

ABOUT THE ILLUSTRATOR:
Sharon Lane Holm has been drawing pictures her entire life. She has been a children's book illustrator for many years. Sharon lives in New Fairfield, Connecticut. She paints with fluid acrylics and adds colored pencil.